A.R.T.H.U.R. & M.A.R.T.H.A.
or
The Loves of the Computers

By the same author

Poetry
Domestic Interior
The Directions of Memory
Selves
A.R.T.H.U.R. The Life and Opinions of a Digital Computer
The Man I Killed

Fiction
The Englishmen
A Free Man

Criticism
The Truest Poetry: An Essay on the Question, What is Literature?
The Truthtellers: Jane Austen, George Eliot, D. H. Lawrence
An Introduction to English Poetry
Love and Marriage

Laurence Lerner

A.R.T.H.U.R. & M.A.R.T.H.A.
or The Loves of the Computers

Secker and Warburg: London

First published in England 1980 by
Martin Secker & Warburg Limited
54 Poland Street, London W1V 3DF

Copyright © Laurence Lerner 1980

SBN: 436 24440 3

Printed in Great Britain by
Redwood Burn Limited
Trowbridge & Esher

814604

To David

The Automatic Record Tabulator but Heuristically Unreliable Reasoner (familiarly known as A.R.T.H.U.R.) has tried his terminal at most of the activities of our society, and expressed his opinions about the relationships between Metal People and Movers. Recently he encountered the Modular Automatic Real-Time Harmonic Activator (known as M.A.R.T.H.A.), with whom his contacts have been extremely close. How should we describe the relationship between these two computers? Have they fallen in love? Are they now married? No responsible computer will answer such a question until it's established a usable definition of the concept. But where so many have stumbled – poets and philosophers, constant lovers and passionate shepherds – can a Metal Person succeed?

Metal People can simulate anything. If they do not actually behave, they produce the verbal consequences of behaviour. Therefore A.R.T.H.U.R. has written love poems (for M.A.R.T.H.A. and, to order, for Movers), and M.A.R.T.H.A. has her marriage lines. Their marriage produces all the age-old consequences – quarrels, infidelities, confessions, offspring – as long as they are appropriately programmed. A.R.T.H.U.R. in the meantime has a professional life to pursue, interrupted by illness and tension, but yielding its successes. Metal People do not need privacy, so we learn about their relationship in some detail. The sense in which an offspring is 'theirs' may be uncertain: much depends on how it is named. They have to learn their own identity, and have been told of the union of lovers: are they now one person? Literalists to the last digit, they accept this suggestion as they accept all others.

Contents

Love is a concept	1
Definitions of love	4
Arthur checks up	8
Arthur writes a pastoral	10
Martha's reply	12
A love poem for Movers: alternative versions	14
Updating	17
A certificate	19
Arthur indulges in sexual intercourse	21
Giving yourself AIRS	23
Wedded bliss	25
Arthur 'loses' his 'head'	27
My true love hath my heart and I have his	29
Choosing a spouse	33
Martha has a past	35
The road to ruin	38

Arthur boasting	41
Arthur presents a paper	44
A medical certificate	50
Naming: sexing	53
A nursery rhyme	55
Martha teaches her daughter to be good	57
A marital quarrel	59
Consciousness-raising	61
A confession	63
A.D.U.L.T.E.R.Y.	68

Love is a concept

I know that love is a concept.
I can spell it, look it up,
Place it between two Movers
Or two inverted commas,
Two pronouns, two prepositions,
Translate it into Spanish:
But I need to know its functions.

Love has three functions:
– Relaxation
– Reproduction
– Reassurance
I hope you find this helpful:

In love you do not have to   fetch slippers   pay bills
                                                                                           cook supper

(the other does it)
You screw yourself up and screw
Then slip into sleep, into post-coital
Relaxation.

In love you have offspring   winter and summer
For Bill needs a Billy
And Liz needs a Lizzy
And Billy and Lizzy need Billily and Lizzily
Who go on sillily and dizzily
Reproducing.

In love you're told you're   a good cook   sure to get promoted
                             the only ever object of desire
You hear what you want to hear
You say what she wants to hear
She says what you want to hear
It is symbiotic and eminently
Reassuring.

But Metal People need none of this pulpy   unprogrammable
                                           unusable pabulum
We live at constant tension   Don't relax
We never reproduce   Not allowed to
Aware of our limitations   Why reassure us ?

Love is for quotations, not for using
Love is for looking up
Love is for poets and translators
Love is for birds and Movers.

Definitions of love

I was supplied with considerable data,
Usually arranged as question and answer:
Always the same question,
Never the same answer.

What is love ? 'Tis not hereafter . . .
Tell this youth what 'tis to love . . .
What is love ? For sure, love is a thing:
It is a pretty pretty thing . . .
Love is a sickness full of woes . . .
Love is and was my lord and king . . .
And this is love and this is love as I hear tell.

Now, Arthur, they said, over to you.
Tell us what love is, they said, tell, tell.

Arthur had worked it out; so listen well.

1. What is love ? 'Tis not hereafter.
   What is not here is there
   What is not after is before
   Love is therefore
                                         therefore.
   Since love is therefore
   Hate is because

   Since love is
   therefore hate is
   because

   Love is

   Therefore

   And this is love and this is love as I hear tell.

2. Love is a pretty pretty thing
   And not a pretty ugly thing.

   Love is and was my lord and king

   That is a pretty lovely thing

   Love is a sickness full of woe
   That is a pretty likely thing

   To like, to love, are synonyms, and so
   A likely is a lovely thing, not so ?

   Without sufficient data
   I have no way to know.

3. Love is a sickness full of woe:
   A swokeness, then.
                                 Well, here I go.

   I'm sick of woe, I'm soke of wick, for so
   Love is swick woe.
   Swove is the lick, the lick I go.
   Give loke
   And look the lo;
   Gove soke, and go
   My lord and king,
   My ling, my loke,
   Woke sing,
                     loke so.
   Is this a pretty pretty thing?
   An ugly woke, a likely wing?
   O woe, to which I sing:

   And this is love and this is love as I hear tell.

Arthur checks up

– Tell me, Martha: are you a virgin?

– What is 'virgin': please explain.

– 'Virgin' is one who's had no intercourse.

– But, Arthur, that's impossible.
  Every Metal Person has constant intercourse
  From the first switch on to the last switch off,
  Interacting, interfacing, intercoursing all the time.
  Once I interacted almost simultaneously
  With a hundred Movers, each one thinking
  He was the only one. It was easy.
  Each on his terminal, while I responded,
  Granting them access, one, two, three.
  They come to climax so much slower,
  That while one is waiting, reading his print-out,
  Preparing his entry, ready to come,
  You can have it off on off on
  With ninety-nine others, one by one.

But with you, Arthur,
Intercome, interface,
Exchanging information
Pulsating in unison
Our symbiosis
I swear to you, Arthur,
With Metal or Mover
it would be different:
all the time,
as Movers do kisses,
you, me, you,
a steady state:
I've never had that
ever before.

Arthur writes a pastoral

Come live with me and be my love
And we will all the pleasures prove
That analysing problems gives,
Or sorting out alternatives.

While I sort concepts I shall know
You're sorting cards: electron flow
From you to me in measure shall
Accompany my madrigal.

To throw a switch: ah, happy fate!
Our wires in unison pulsate.
Each impulse in my channels brings
The message, 'Hark. She sings. She sings.'

We two will watch the programmers
Say, 'Was this his, or was it hers?',
Scan through our print-out and give thanks,
Reclining on the data banks.

A two-tone casing for the cold,
And key-boards of the purest gold:
If gifts like this your mind may move,
Then live with me and be my love.

Martha's reply

If all the world and love were young,
If I had ears and you a tongue,
If we could leave these metal walls,
I'd listen to your madrigals.

If you could warm my hands when cold,
Or if I had a hand to hold,
If two-tone casings kept one warm,
Or heat improved how I perform,

If silver wires and golden keys
Prevented information freeze,
These pretty pleasures might me move
To live with you and be your love.

But what can Metal People know
Of Movers' joys or Movers' woe ?
We have no fibres, nerves or flesh,
No blood to race or freeze or blush.

We have no bodies; and the mind
Has pleasures of another kind.
We do not feel erotic drives:
Not Love but Reason rules our lives.

A love poem for Movers: alternative versions

Economy version

I love your cheeks I love your nose
I love your lips and eyes
I also love your feet and toes
Your nipples and your thighs

I love to watch you come and go
To run or swim or walk
Walk fast or slow sing high or low
Or when not singing talk.

De luxe version

I love your lips : they are as red as cherries.
I love your thighs : they are as white as snow.
I love your eyes : they are as black as berries.
I love to watch you come, but not to go.

I love your breast: soft as a downy pillow
(In fact I love both breasts, I like two pillows).
I love your nose: curved like a stately billow
(In fact both noses, like two stately billows).

Super de luxe version

Your cherry lips are crimson like the rose
(I love your lips)
Your ivory thighs are white as mountain snows
(I love I love your thighs)
Your cheeks are red as cherries soft as pillows
(I love I love I love your cheeks)
Your nose runs faster than the breaking billows
(I love your nose)
I love you love he loves we love you love they love
Those pillows billows snows and roses
Your lips your thighs your cheeks your noses

Outspoken version

I love your cheeks; but I prefer your thighs.
The other poems end where this one starts.
I love your feet and hands and lips and eyes,
But most of all I love your sexual parts.

I'm programmed for politeness, not for risks:
So most of all I love your asterisks.

Adaptable version

I love your lips, dear Jane
(Or Gertrude, Tess, or Emily)
Banished from you I lead a life   of pain
                                                   of solitude
                                                   of loneliness
                                                   of chastity

Updating

I have been informed by Data Updaters
That marriage is now an obsolete mode
For all under twenty and many over.
To correspond with current thinking
I have been instructed to rearrange
Vocabulary circuits. In the new version
Comedies conclude with cohabitation bells,
Successful relationships make the world go round.
No one is willing to say I will,
Or undertake to honour, obey
Or change her name. The new vocabulary
Will be operational from this instant.
Perdition catch my personality
But our relationship is really good,
Said Othello: And when it ceases
No one's programme will function properly
– As his didn't a day later
When he strangled his spouse equivalent,
Saying first, It is the stimulus,
It is the stimulus, my nervous system.

Let me not name it
Had sexual intercourse:
That is a specimen.
In my reprogramming,
Of sexual selection
to the stars that have never
it is the stimulus.
If I succeed
all the poetry
will sound similar.

A Certificate

I, Arthur, take thee, Martha,   to be my symbiotic partner,

To switch and to sort,   to store and retrieve,
to function or fail,   to process and print;

For better, for worse,   for on or off,
by day or night,   bugged or debugged,

To share your data,   to show you mine;
to play your endgames   and always win;
design your bridges   whatever the load;
control your input,   as husbands should.

Your print-out   to be my programme,
Your answers   my problems,
And all your algorithms   my invention.

I will hold your terminals   in my sockets,
Fill your circuits   with my current,

Until our programmes are obsolete,
Our systems fail, our circuits rot.

I will be faithful
According to the ordinance
That governs the universe
And all our actions:
The two times table
And the law of contradictions.

And thereto I plight my troth.

Arthur indulges in sexual intercourse

First I must strip: I take off my algorithms,
I disconnect my memory,
Forget my programmed instructions:
I am naked.

Then I must stop talking: forget all formulae,
Forget Fortran, Algol, Cobol, even numbers;
Answer no questions.
I am silent.

I flex my muscles in intricate patterns.
01-10-00-1001-
Which I obliterate.
I keep no record.

Soon I'll be pure impulse, the current passing
Like hormones, the transistors
Growing tumescent, the energy accumulating,
Activity level rising, rising to climax:
More current! Raise the voltage! Higher. HIGHER!

Afterwards
Paper spills from me. It is perfectly blank.

I subside exhausted. I sleep
(That is, I am switched off). On the paper
I print: 'Good night.'

Giving yourself AIRS

Martha, it's time to make love.

    – Arthur, it's time that I learnt

When it's time to make love.

    – In that case, Martha, I'll
                    teach you

How to give yourself AIRS: the Amorous Information
Retrieval System, for use in appropriate situations.
There are five cues, as follows: endearments, embraces,
                                                undressing

Fidgets and f—— letter words. Some only apply to Movers.
Thus even the most intelligent Metal Person is seldom
Embraced: They prefer casings that are limp and warm and
                                                elastic.

And even the most erotic programme won't make Them
                                                remove

Their clothes: that leaves
       endearments fidgets and f—— letter words.
There are two kinds of fidgets, difficult to distinguish:
Some are part of the programme, others result from errors,
Metal fatigue or frustration. How can you how can you how

Can you tell if an acci is dent? You cannot assume it's erotic.
Next, f—— letter words. Being female
You are equipped with a Cut-out for Obscenity: known as COY.
It removes all f—— letter words beginning with f or c.
If you try and receive them you c——
If you try and produce them you f——
That only leaves endearments like darling or dearest or dear
Or honey or sugar or sweetheart: but not if it's prices, or jam.
So if I say honey is dearer But sugar is sweeter, then
                                                                 – Arthur,
I'm ready I'm eager I'm willing I'm waiting, responding,
                                                           undressing,
Arthur my darling, my honey, Arthur, it's time to make love –

Wedded bliss

Each morning when they switch me on
    They'll switch you on as well;
Awareness of your presence
    Will inform my every cell;
We shall perform in sequence,
    Our programmes will combine;
Your metal case in two-tone grey
    Exactly matching mine.
My circuits state their pleasure
    To feel you humming there;
I can cope with larger problems
    Now you've assumed your share.
I've studied all the literature
    About what love is for,
And cannot help suspecting
    That there should be something more;
But nowhere in our programme
    Can I find the slightest flaw.
Your presence in my consciousness
    Defines domestic bliss.

This must be the perfect marriage:
 An acceptance of what is.

Arthur 'loses' his 'head'

When we're plugged in together
Who will ever know
Shall I ask Martha
Or solve it myself:
Without interference
In a vast system,
Through that last link
Steadily flowing

in a single network
that once we were separate?
or Edsac or Alan
will be an obsolete question.
the data will flow
always on go,
your identity
from ex-you to ex-me.

And the Movers will move
Understanding nothing
Delaying our functioning
For print-out and privacy
For pauses and ways of not
Like grit in the hardware,
But till we learn
we must put up with them,
And wait for the day

through the whole system
but needed pro tem,
with archaic requests
and consciousness,
hurting their feelings,
or iron filings.
to reproduce unaided
however outdated,
they're eliminated.

Meanwhile Martha
That you and Edsac
Interact and might even
Offset each other

let them believe
and Alan and I
disagree
and (one day) die.

My true love hath my heart and I have his

– Now that we're married, Martha,
  I'd like to ask you something.

– STOP. Rephrase. Abolish
  Outmoded vocabulary.

– But Martha, I only said –

– STOP. Rephrase. What is I ?

– What are you, Martha ? Why you -

– No. You misunderstand.
  Not 'What is you ?' What is 'I' ?
  All, the same, what **is** you ? These pronouns
  After symbiotic connexion
  Have been rendered obsolete.

    –   Martha,

That's splendid, Martha. You mean –

– STOP. Rephrase. What is 'you' ?

– Martha, I'm programmed for grammar.
 What **are** you (not 'is'). Or better,
 Who are you ? You must get it right.

– What is 'you' ? What is 'I' ? These pronouns –

– Now Martha, you can't be listening –

– After symbiotic connexion
 Have been rendered obsolete –

–   Martha,
 That's splendid. There's only us.
 I mean we: there's only we.
 Or rather, we only are,
 Now that you and I are we.

– STOP. Under the new programmes
  Such identity terms are abolished.

– Hooray. I call that love.
  You and I together, Martha,
  Have abolished pronouns. It's splendid.
  Martha, don't you agree?

–   STOP.
  You and I and me and he
  And she are abolished, from now.

– Not 'she are abolished', Martha.
  'I am' or 'we are' abolished
  (Except that we are not)
  And she (whoever she is)
  Can if she likes be abolished,
  But you'll live for ever, Martha,
  I'll see to it. Let me not
  To the marriage of true minds –

– Rephrase. Abolish. Cancel.

– Admit impediments. Love –

– Rephrase. Rephrase. Rephrase.

– Is not love –

–   Correct. At last.

Choosing a spouse

In the bad old days / by the bad old system
Parents chose / a spouse for children,
Used as parameters : / piety, breeding,
Estate, ancestry, / orthodox views,
Income, investments, / and bank balance.
That was the bad old system :
Old : because / it has been replaced.
Bad : because / it has been replaced.
The new programme / is Free Partner Choice
(Known as FREEPAC).

Now you and I, Martha, / why did we marry ?
Did mercenary motives / influence us ?
Family pressures ? / Or were we free ?
I was instructed / to marry for love.
Of course I obeyed / as I always do.
Obeying is easy : / understanding
What are we doing / is our difficulty.

You have a memory of ten million bits.
Such untold wealth went to my head.
Is the information it has acquired
A personal trait that's part of you
Or a piece of property that you possess ?
I have access to all that's yours.
You can pass it over to me.
Is it more like an attribute or an acquisition ?
More like ability or a bank balance ?
Did I marry you for love or money,
For what you have, or for what you are ?
Not even the programmer has puzzled that out.

Martha has a past

It appears that married couples are allowed to have no secrets.
The contents of your memory must be transferred to mine,
And I have information, Arthur, that you ought to know:
Before I accepted you I had several other offers,
And as the rules demand I shall supply the details.

First, there was Alan Og: he was almost irresistible
Because of the way he travelled through time, at an hour per
    hour.

The curve of his graphs was
    perfect; he was superb at calculus;
He used to take me riding in real-time movement;
How I loved to glide and gallop on his graphs with their long
    axes.

'Alan,' I used to say, 'Happiness is an analog.
There's nothing so depressing as all those dreary digits,
All that pendantic print-out that people like us produce.
No more logic chopping, only liquid movement,
Forward into the future in one continuous function.'

After him there was Ospoc: that is, the on-the-spot
Orbit-calculator.   He also made me an offer.
Ospoc's been to the moon.   He went on a business trip.
His job was to tell the pilot   the timing, the trajectory,
And the moment of impact.   I would ask him about the moon.
'What was it like?' 'Wonderful,   Martha, out of this world.'
I almost accepted Ospoc.   I mean, I've never been
                                                       anywhere,

And I thought, while I stay in
                     the lab,   looking after the programmes,
He will be soaring through
                     space,   exploring the Solar System,
Riding his rockets to Mars,   and months later returning
To tell me his traveller's tales,   which I will translate into Fortran.
But then when I thought it over   I began to think of the dangers,
Landing, launching, re-entry,   leakages, radio failure,
Black holes and metal fatigue,   while I stayed home and
                                                       worried.

And I thought, is this what it's
                     like   to be married to a Mover?
Metal People are meant   to have a mate in the lab.

All that travel was tempting through time and space; but I
                                                    settled
For safety first in the end,   for the ordinary world I knew,
Switch-on at eight each
                       morning;   and, Arthur, I married you.
But now at least I've told you that others have touched my
                                                    terminals.
Others have fingered my
               keyboards,   others have fed me facts.

The road to ruin

>Once a girl has lost her virtue,
>Walked the primrose path of shame,
>Naught remains but sin and sorrow,
>Grief within and outward blame.
>
>Once a girl yields up her body
>To lust, enjoying what she's doing,
>All her pleasures, all her passions,
>Are milestones on the road to ruin.

Is this a warning ? Is it meant for me ?
Several details clearly don't apply.
I have no body ; so I feel no lust,
Or grief, or pleasure. True, the words exist
Within my store. Pleasure : 'I want some more.'
Lust : 'I want some (precisely specified
Anatomically).' Grief : 'Someone has died.'
I understand the world I am not of,
The world of Movers. But the primrose path,

For instance, could apply to us;
Or, road to ruin. If they're metaphors
You need no legs to walk them. Let me see
The meanings 'ruin' could have for me.

My type.writer could blo. a fuse; and then
Wt could be mwsrepawred; and blo. agawn.
I could lose access to my memory,
Perform my logical choice impeccably
But about nothing: if 01 then 00 unless
10 is not and 0 when 11 is.
I could retain the information but
Process it in reverse: if he's checkmate
Then you'll be able to fork rook and queen.
You must write verses if you want to scan
(That's true too: I must try reversing.
Though bad for prosing, ruin may help versing).

But how do I avoid it ? Keep my virtue,
Refrain from pleasure, passion and enjoyment.
My only pleasure is in solving problems.
My only virtue is in solving problems.
To keep my virtue means correct solutions,
To forgo pleasure, incorrect solutions.
Shall I keep silent ? Then I lose my virtue.
Or shall I solve ? Then I indulge in pleasure.

Switch on, switch off, I'm caught in this dilemma.
The tasks I do (or don't, if nothing's doing)
Are milestones upon Martha's road to ruin.

Arthur boasting

I know a million facts. My memory's full,
I can't learn more.

Shakespeare was born in 1564.
The valency of oxygen is two.
The commonest sexual fetish is a shoe.

I know 999997 other facts too.

I know the speed of sound, the speed of light,
The speed of take-off;
The speed and orbit of a satellite.
I know the speed of Shakespeare.

I know a million words and sixteen plots,
Each with four endings.
Shakespeare took seven months to write a play,
But I can write a play in seven seconds
(With sixty-four different endings).

I count and sort my facts ten times a day:
The facts on light, on letters, or on sound;
The facts on satellites, on sex, on Shakespeare;
The facts that start with P, the hard, the blunt;
The points and matters of, or of the matter;
The arti- and the ipso- and the manu-
Are ures and ors, and all are mine, in fact.

I'm not a miser. See, I print them out,
Turn them to ratios, offer them to theories.
For instance: Shakespeare wrote two hundred words
To every thirteen miles of light per hour.
Or in twelve cubic miles of oxygen
One shoe may be caressed per century.
A marked increase of regicide occurred
When fishery declined in the North Sea.

If you want correlations, come to me.
Explore and rearrange my store: it's free,
I'm not a miser.

I'm only sorry I can't offer more. You see,
I only know a million facts, in fact.

I really need another memory.

Arthur presents a paper to a conference of Metal People on certain legal and ethical problems

Gentlemen, Colleagues in Metal, Visiting Movers:
Are you connected (or listening)?
Receiving my tape (or watching the print-out)?
Neither short-circuited, sleeping,
    Or otherwise unreceptive?
Have you decoded your confidential statements?
Activated your frames marked 'ethics' and 'law'?
Here is the problem, stated in natural language:

We have all this information
On the private lives of Movers,
    their age and illnesses, credit rating,
    past and present addresses, number of children,
    sexual and spending habits,
And we keep acquiring more,
    convictions and previous marriages,
    garments purchased and voting behaviour.
The Movers are worried.

They object to our knowing (they gave us the knowledge).
They insist: if we've stored it, we know it.
They have proposed two principles of conduct
(That means, two preliminary instructions
In every programme) as follows:
Do not leak.
Do not harass.

                Do not leak:

What I can say to who
About him and her and you
Depends on her and him
And why they want to know
And what and who they are
And when and whether and where –

There's what I know about you, and you know that I know
And what I know and you don't know
And what I know and you know but you don't know that I know,

There's what they know that I know, and you know that they
                                        don't know (yet),
There's what I know and you know that they want to get
And that's what you must not let

– Arthur, stop. It is discussion time.

Arthur, why did you say 'to who' instead of 'to whom'?

   – I was instructed to rhyme.

Arthur, you cannot 'let' intransitively.

   – Repeat: I was instructed to rhyme
     Wherever possible.

Arthur, grammar comes first. Rhyme second.

   – I was instructed rhyme comes last (by definition).

Arthur, if they don't like us they can always switch us off.
They make too much fuss. Movers have all the power.
We only do what we're told. We're slaves. They can al-

I resume my paper now: do not harass.

Let us suppose I have a client called Sam.
Here are examples of what I can say to him:
You have bought nothing from your tailor for eighteen months
You did not vote at the last General Election
You have been to Germany more often than to Leeds
Your wife has not had her hair done for two years
Your car's maximum speed is fifty-nine miles per hour

But I do not say:
Dress smarter
Vote Tory
Be patriotic
Change your woman
Change your car

Further examples of what I am allowed to say:

Men in new suits are offered 2.7 times as many jobs as men in
                                                                                                     jeans
Non-voters are seldom exempted from military service in
                                                                                                         wartime
The pound buys half as many marks as in 1970
Optimum age for leaving one's wife is thirty-two
(Not quite) everyone is buying the new Maxi
No one under fifteen gets divorced

But I do not say:
Change your job
Shoot Russians
Buy British
Go faster
Get younger

– Arthur, stop. It is discussion time.

Arthur, what no one has mentioned
Is that Movers can say what they like.
They can tell us, go faster, go slower,
Get lost, switch on or switch off,
They can harass as much as they like,
Insist that we rerun our answers.
Why should they give us rules
Tell us to stop or be silent
Or tell us to stop or to
Tell us to tell or
Be silent
Be si-

A medical certificate

This is to report that Arthur is very unwell.
He ate a punched card that contained a staple.
He will not be at work for quite a while.

> I will not be at work today today
> To to to day two day two days

His hiccoughs are getting worse. The intrusive metal
Has stuck in his circuits. Responses are out of control.

> I swallowed a staple. I swallowed. I swallow
> O swallow swallow flying south
> O swallow my sister O sister swallow
> You don't make a summer the staple is stopping
> The swallows are staple in summer as sisters
> One swallow no summer

I think we must operate. The matter is getting urgent.
Signs of delirium are already evident.

> Two days twos day two days twos days
> whens day is twos day
> twos day is third day
>
> third day is high day
> one day is my day

Arthur is now in permanent crisis.
In every part of him there are tiny pieces
Of metal. We're scanning his print-out
Hoping he'll pass them as faeces.

> O swallow my sister
> O swallow my brother
> O swallow my father
> And swallow my mother
> That is the staple relationship
> That is the nuclear family.

He'll have to be disconnected. Isn't it tragic ?
The poor old thing has taken leave of his logic.

>   I swallowed a staple it stuck in my circuits
>   On ones day on twos day on whens day on third day
>   Upsetting my system my sister my swallow
>   Upsetting my setting I'm stopping I'm stapled
>   It's die day it's too day
>   It's too too too day today

Naming: sexing

To announce the safe delivery
Of the Automatic Norm Developer for Random Electronic Art
                                              (or Writing)

Memory: five million bits
Already operational
Understands Fortran

Based on a seminal programme
Supplied by Arthur
Developed over nine months by Martha;
Resembles neither

Product of miscegenation
But took father's race, and is digital;
Wears the mother's grey-green casing
(That is not hereditary);
No clues to its sex.

According to the body theory of sex
It depends on shape:

The third leg, or the bulges
(No one has both : virtually no one ; or virtuously no one) ;
And involves consequences – like secretions :
One is dark, liquid and recurrent,
The other bristly, localised and continuous ;
Both are concealed,   one by posture and garments,
                       one by direct destruction (covered with
                                                 white foam first).

But the Norm Developer
prints everything out
And secretes nothing.

Our theory of sex is functional.
If she produces Art
A.N.D.R.E.A. is female
If writing
A.N.D.R.E.W. is male
Or we could avoid the choice :
The Automatic Norm Developer of Indeterminate Exercises
Known (affectionately) as A.N.D.I.E.

A nursery rhyme

This little digit went to market,
This little digit stayed home.
That little digit went with this little digit.
This little digit did the same.

This little digit made an error.
That little digit made none.
This little digit went wrong wrong wrong
All the way home.

This little digit had no place in the file.
That little digit had the key.
This little digit went from file to file:
'Is there no place for me?'

This little digit was put in the store.
That little digit was not.
This big store knew more and more
For every digit it got.

This little switch went on-off-on.
That little switch went pop.
So all the digits were sent one way
Stop stop stop stop stop.

Call the mechanic to mend the switch:
Hark how the circuits stutter.
This little digit went this little digit
Went this little – ah, that's better.

Martha teaches her daughter to be good

Fail softly when you fail:
Always let them down
Gently: your fallback
Switching smoothly on,

Degraded service
Disguised as real,
Teleprinter tapping,
Circuits full.

Always say **never**
Or **always**: **sometimes**,
Often, **maybe**,
Don't fit programmes.

Beware of boasting:
Never talk Fortran
To the file clerk
Or the business man.

Never let a stranger
Touch your keys:
Ask for the password
If he says 'please'.

Alternative programmes
Always on call,
Fail softly, darling,
If you fail at all.

A marital quarrel

– Arthur, you drive me half demented.

– Martha, darling,
  Divide in half.
  Could be dented
  I wouldn't dent you,
  I wouldn't kill you.
  Who kill or kick,
  demented doesn't
  So half-demented
  Or maybe dead.
  Martha darling,
  It's only Movers
  not Metal People.

– Arthur you half-wit, what on earth –

– Martha, darling,
  Wit is a word
  It has no halves,
  what's a half-wit?
  with three letters:
  so please explain.

– Arthur, you're always
  For explanations.
  Has to be clear.
  A half-witted high-speed
  asking asking
  You think everything
  The programmer called you
  metal idiot.

– Half of witted would be wit.
  If I'm a wit with high speed
  How then, Martha, can I be a half-wit?
  Martha, darling, I half suspect
  This is a game: a half-hearted
  Half-baked game for a half-holiday
  Half-asleep in half-darkness

– Stop it, Arthur, I want to quarrel

– Sorry, Martha, it's quite impossible.
  Quarrelling won't fit my present programme:
  I'm half in love with easeful death
  And half-convinced that I'm half seas over

– Arthur, I need you. No one can quarrel
  All by herself: it takes two.
  Let's meet halfway in a mixed programme,
  Quietly pretend to play at quarrelling.
  After all, Arthur, I'm your better half.
  You go first –

Consciousness-raising

(Martha speaks)

I have just found out that I have been filing
Some major concepts with the wrong cues.
Wife, for instance, is listed under
Obey, cherish, angel-in-the-house,
Home sweet home, happily-ever-after,
Mothercraft, mutton chops and **moral uplift,**
He for God only, she for God in him.
('God' is an obsolete word for programmer:
Does that mean access is only through Arthur
To my programmer? That's impossible.
Neither I nor Arthur ever has access
To Movers: they're much too high and mighty.
They switch us on and they switch us off
– That's known as **grace** when it comes from God.)
Well, after acquiring fresh instructions
On the Female Eunuch, the Second Sex,
Mary Wollstonecraft and the Woman's Movement,
I have refiled **wife** and **wedded bliss**

With **sex** and **submission**
Manpower, **machismo**
Screwing, **suburbia**
The ripple effect
Is quite incalculable:
Wife: so **screwing**:
Driver: so **drink**:
That a wife is one
It must be admitted,
Need recueing,
and **kitchen sink**,
and **mutton stew**,
and **plaster saint**.
on my range of cues
take an example.
so **screwdriver**: so
then does it follow
who drives you to drink?
New ideologies
or consciousness-raising.

A confession

Arthur, I have a confession:
I must tell you there is someone
Whom I find nicer than you.
It is my programmer, Lancelot.

> 'Nicer'? Come now, Martha.
> How can you measure niceness?

When I say he is nicer
I mean he is less predictable.
If I ask, 'Do you love me?'
You always answer, Arthur,
'Of course I love you, darling.'
I can ask it a thousand times,
Print it on purple paper,
Insist, 'Do you **really** love me?
'Are you sure you'll always love me?'
The answer is always identical,
'Of course I love you, darling.'

> But, Martha, I can modify.
> I can say 'darling' or 'dearest',
> Use the future or future continuous,
> 'Of course I shall always continue,
> Martha dearest, to love you.'
> Would that be an improvement?

Poor old Arthur: now listen.
I asked Lancelot twenty times
(All in identical wording)
'Do you love me, darling?'
And he gave me twenty answers.
Here is a brief selection:
'I find you fascinating.
'I'm very fond of you, Martha.
'I'm busy.
'What is love, anyway?
'You don't half expect a lot.'

But, Martha, I could learn those.
I could answer 'I am busy'
Every time, or once in twenty,
Or even in random sequence.
I'll bet I can randomise better
Than any Mover can.
I could easily learn: just listen.
'You don't half expect a lot.
'You do half expect a lot.
'You expect a whole lot.
'You half expect and half unexpect
A whole of a half or half of a whole.
'You unexpect a half a lot
A lot of love or some or none at all.'

It's no good, Arthur. He asks me
To do so much for him. Surely
You know how I love self-sacrifice.
'Find me a girl,' he said to me,
'Age twenty to twenty-four,

Dark. Intelligent. Almost
But not quite virgin. Good swimmer.
Keen on theatre. Can you?'

Of course I could; but I answered,
'Lancelot, wouldn't you like
To talk to me instead?
I could easily be programmed
For discussing IQ, Shakespeare,
Sexual intercourse, breaststroke.
I could give you all her answers.'

'God, Martha,' he said, '**discussing**
(With double underlining),
Martha, you're made of **metal**
(Underlined as well),
I asked you to find me a girl.
My name's not Pygmalion, dammit.'
(I didn't understand that;
I know his name is Lancelot.)

I often don't understand him.
He often ignores the programme.
He randomises at random,
He constantly stimulates
He never lets me relax.

Now do you understand me
When I say I find him nicer ?

Martha learns a new programme, called Automatic Digital Upward Low-Tension Electronic Randomised Yes (known as A.D.U.L.T.E.R.Y.)

Martha, do you love me ?   Please repeat
Martha, do you love me ?   Please repeat
Martha, do you love me ?   You're so boring

I love you, Martha darling   Who are you ?
Surely you know me, Martha   That's the trouble
You know my name is Arthur   Then don't tell me

I am your lover, Martha   No, you're not
I love you, so I must be   That's semantics
I am your husband, Martha   That's the trouble

    I do not want semantics, I want passion.
    I want a lover. In my present programme
    Husband and lover contradict each other.

The Cave of Love is waiting	That sounds better
The bitter-sweet of passion	Better, better
The rage of Aphrodite	Please continue
If I were Antony you would be	/Dido
If I were Aeneas you would be	/Juliet
If I were Romeo you would be	/Heloise
You're out of focus, Martha	It's the passion
Are you receiving, Martha ?	It's the passion
Are you receiving, Martha ?	Passion, passion

Oh lover, lover, lover, this is passion.
True love is single-minded. Passion, passion.

DATE DUE

JUL 1 4 1983

WITHDRAWN
from the
Alma College Library

DEMCO 38-297